Titles in the series

First published in Great Britain 1986 by
Hamish Hamilton Children's Books
27 Wrights Lane, London W8 5SL
Copyright © 1986 (text) by Julie Fitzpatrick
Copyright © (illustrations) by Diana Bowles
All rights reserved

British Library Cataloguing in Publication Data
Fitzpatrick, Julie
Bounce, stretch and spring.–(Science spirals)
1. Elasticity–Juvenile literature
2. Plasticity–Juvenile literature
I. Title II. Series
620.1′123 TA418

ISBN 0-241-11723-2
Printed in Spain

20817

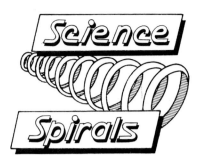

Bounce, Stretch and Spring

Julie Fitzpatrick

Illustrated by Diana Bowles

Hamish Hamilton · London

Equipment you need for experiments in this book

Stretchy things: *anything which will stretch*

Stretching tights: *pair of tights, round stones*

A springy elastic toy *and* How strong is elastic?: *two kinds of thin elastic, plasticine, weighing machine, weights*

Stretching rubber bands: *rubber bands, 2 yoghurt pots, string, paper clips, marbles (you need at least 25) or large nails*

Things with springs *and* Make a springy toy: *thin wire, pen, straight stick, cotton reel, plasticine*

Making weighing machines: *rubber band, yoghurt pot, paper, Blutack, large spring from a chair or mattress, 2 tins that will fit one inside the other, things to weigh*

Clips and grips: *anything which will grip, metal and plastic paper clips, bull dog clip*

Stretching your body: *wire, cotton reels, pieces of sponge, sellotape*

Springy air: *balloon, balloon pump, felt tip pen*

Bouncing balls (pp. 20–25): *a variety of balls, tray, ping pong ball, marble*

Making sounds: *rubber bands, 2 containers which will not bend, piece of rubber sheeting or balloon, pencils*

Springy power: *washing-up liquid bottle, scissors, 2 pencils, long rubber band*

Contents

Stretchy things

Are you wearing anything that is stretchy?
Collect some of these things.

Pull them and see which ones stretch.
Some things stretch and spring back into shape.
What happens when you pull these things?

They stretch but do not spring back.
Some things do not stretch at all.
Test some more things.
Sort them into sets.

	stretch
spring	
do not spring	

Stretching tights

A pair of tights are stretchy.
How far will they stretch?
Put a stone into one leg of a pair of
tights. (Do not use sharp stones as
these will ladder the tights.)
Can you make the leg bounce?

Put in more stones, one by one.
How far does the leg stretch?
Take out the stones. Does the leg
spring back into shape?

5

A springy elastic toy

Elastic will stretch and spring. It can be used in clothes. It stretches to let you in, then springs back to grip you.

Make a springy elastic toy.

YOU NEED

thin elastic
plasticine
paper for decoration

WHAT YOU DO

1. Cut a length of elastic.
Make a ball of plasticine and fix it to one end of the elastic.
See how the plasticine bounces.

2. Cut another length of elastic the same as the first.
Onto this, fix a larger ball of plasticine.

3. Start the two balls bouncing at the same time.
Which bounces faster?
Decorate the plasticine to make a toy.

6

How strong is elastic?

There are different kinds of elastic for different jobs. Elastic can be used to keep a jumper in shape. It needs to be thin and strong.

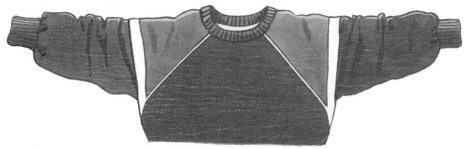

Get two different types of thin elastic. How could you test which is the stronger?

You could add plasticine to each one until it breaks.
This is called the breaking point.
Weigh each ball of plasticine.
Record the breaking point.

Which elastic is stronger?	
	Breaking point
1st elastic	grammes
2nd elastic	grammes

Stretching rubber bands

Rubber bands are useful for
gripping things.
The rubber bands which you buy in a
packet may be of different lengths
and thicknesses.
How will you know which one is best
for the job?
Will a thin rubber band stretch further
than a thick one?
How could you find out?
You could add weights to the rubber
bands and measure how far they
stretch.

YOU NEED

rubber bands
two yoghurt pots
string
paper clips
marbles or large nails of
the same size

WHAT YOU DO

1. Choose a rubber band to fit tightly
around the top of each pot.

2. Make two handles by tying pieces
of string across the pots. (Push the
rubber band down each pot while you
do this.)

8

3. Take two rubber bands of the same length, one thick and one thin.
Hang them over hooks or a cane.
Fix each handle to the rubber band by using a paper clip.

4. See how many marbles or nails it takes to stretch each rubber band.
Put the same number of marbles or nails in each pot.
Which rubber band stretched further?

Does a long rubber band stretch further than a short one?
To find out, keep the two pots, but exchange one of the rubber bands for two of the same thickness and same size as the first.
Use the first rubber band as it is.
Loop the other two together to make them twice as long.
Put the same number of marbles or nails in each pot.
Are the looped rubber bands still twice as long?
Which rubber bands would you choose to grip these things?

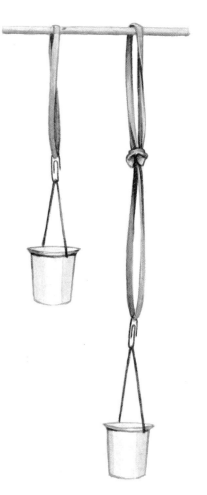

Things with springs

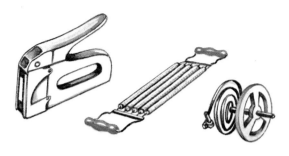

Springs are made from metal.
Most springs are coiled. The metal
is shaped round in rings.
Where have you seen springs
being used?

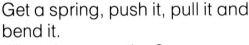

Get a spring, push it, pull it and
bend it.
What do you notice?
It goes back into shape each time.

You can make a spring from a piece of
thin wire.
Wind the wire around a pen.
Take the wire off the pen and feel how
springy it is.
Does it make any difference if the
rings are smaller or closer together?

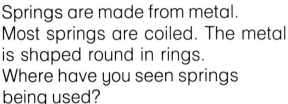

Some electric flexes are coiled. You
pull them out and they spring back.
This is to stop the flex trailing
on the floor.

Make a springy toy

YOU NEED

a straight stick
thin wire
plasticine
a cotton reel

WHAT YOU DO

1. Make a base from plasticine and put in the stick.

2. Use the wire to make a strong spring.

3. Put the spring down over the stick. Press the end of the spring into the plasticine.

4. Drop the cotton reel down the stick to bounce on the spring.
Press the cotton reel down on the spring, then let it go.
How high up the stick will it go?
Fix something at the top of the stick to make a sound as the cotton reel hits it.

Making weighing machines

You can use a rubber band to make a weighing machine.

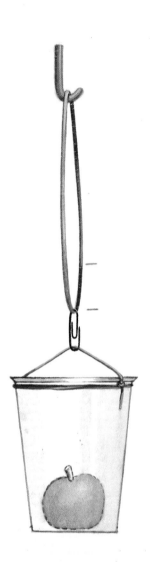

YOU NEED

rubber band
the yoghurt pot, as before
a sheet of paper
Blutack
small packets marked with
their weight

WHAT YOU DO

1. Use the Blutack to stick the paper behind the pot.

2. Put a packet into the pot.
How far does the rubber band stretch?
Get your eyes level with the bottom end of the rubber band.
Put a mark on the paper at this end to show how far the rubber band stretched.
Write the weight of the packet by the mark.

3. Mark the weight of other packets.

4. Now use the weighing machine to find out the weight of any other small objects.

This machine is good for weighing heavier things.

YOU NEED

a large spring from an old chair or mattress
two tins of different sizes: a larger one to take the spring, and a smaller one to fit inside

WHAT YOU DO

1. Put the spring into the larger tin. Put the smaller tin on top of the spring.

2. Put a packet of sugar in the small tin. Mark the small tin at the level of the large tin.

3. Mark the weight of other heavy objects. Can you find anything that weighs about the same as the sugar?

Clips and grips

Springy things are useful for gripping.
Collect some of these things and see
how they work.
Some material can bend and
spring back.

Take three different clips.

Which one is best for gripping two
sheets of paper?
Which one would be best for gripping
two sheets of card?

Which materials feel springy?

Collect some of the materials shown
on the right.
Which ones can be pressed in by
your fingers?
Which ones spring back?

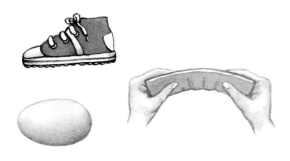

Make a set of materials which cannot
be pressed in.
Sort the other materials like this.

	pressed in
spring back	
do not spring back	

15

Stretching your body

You can bend, stretch and spring.
Your bones do not bend. They need
to be rigid.

Move your fingers up your spine.
The bones which you can feel are
called vertebrae.
If your bones were fixed tightly
together you would not be able
to move.
Between each vertebra is some
spongy material called cartilage.
Make this model of a spine to show
how the cartilage works.

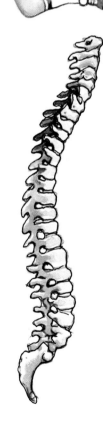

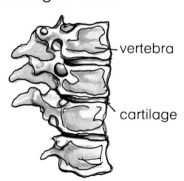

vertebra

cartilage

YOU NEED

a piece of wire for the spine
cotton reels for the vertebrae
bits of sponge for the cartilage
sellotape

WHAT YOU DO

1. First, find how difficult moving would be if your vertebrae were fixed together.
Put some cotton reels on the wire and stick them together with sellotape.
What happens when you try to bend the wire?

2. Take off the sellotape and put some sponge between each vertebrae.
What difference do you notice?

3. The cartilage softens the blow if you sit down or land with a bump.
See what happens when you bang the model down on the table –
    without the sponge
    with the sponge
Cartilage stops the bones crashing together.

Mammals have cartilage between their bones.
It helps them to bounce, stretch and spring.

Springy air

What makes these things springy?

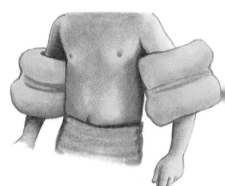

They are filled with air.
Take a balloon and feel how
springy it is.
Use a balloon pump to blow up
the balloon.
Blow it up halfway then let the
pump go.
Can you feel the air pushing back?

How does a balloon change as it is
filled with air?
Write your name on the balloon using
a felt tip pen.
Pump more air into the balloon.
What happens to the letters of
your name?

Let some air out of the balloon.
How do the letters change?
Does the balloon feel more springy
when it is blown up halfway,
or all the way?

Tyres are made of rubber and are
filled with air.
This helps them to bounce over
bumps in the road.

A sharp stone could make a hole in a
tyre. This is called a puncture.
When a tyre has a puncture, air
comes out and the tyre goes flat.

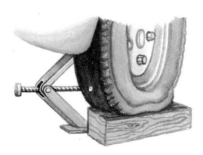

Bouncing balls

Collect as many different balls
as you can.
Do they all bounce?
Drop each one onto the same hard
surface. (The surface is the outside of
an object.)

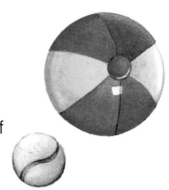

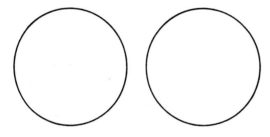

Press your fingers down on a ball
which does not bounce.
Do the same with a ball which
does bounce.
What difference can you feel?

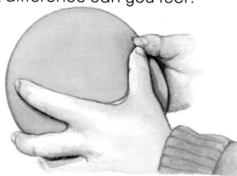

The best bouncer

Take three different balls and find out which is the best bouncer.
To make it fair, you must drop them from the same height.

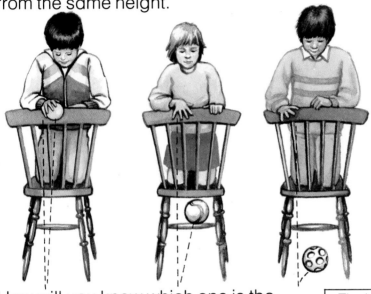

How will you know which one is the best bouncer?

You could –
    count the number of bounces for each ball
    drop them at the same time and see which one bounces for longer.
Why is it best to drop, not throw the balls?

Do the test several times. Put the balls in order, as shown on the right.

The best bouncing ball
1st
2nd
3rd

The best surface for bouncing

Take the best bouncing ball.
It may bounce well on a path, but
will it be as good on grass?
Try it and see.

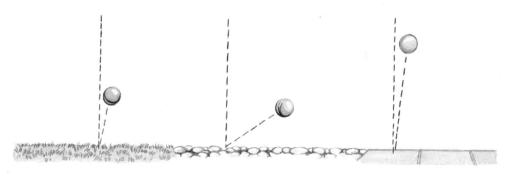

Test the ball on other surfaces.
To make it fair, drop the ball from the
same height each time.
Count the number of bounces and
record what happens.

Which surface is best for bouncing a ball?	
	Number of bounces
path	
grass	
soil	
mud	

A hard surface is best for
bouncing balls.
But what happens if that surface
is bumpy?

Get some stones and put them in a
box or on a tray.
Drop the ball onto them.
In which way (or direction) does the
ball bounce?

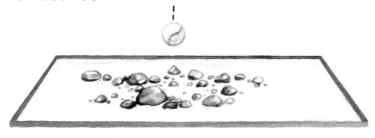

Drop the ball on different stones. Do
this several times.
Can you guess in which direction the
ball will bounce?

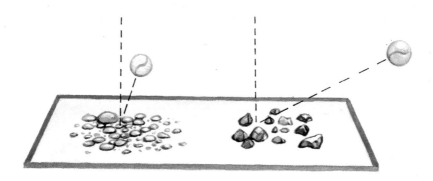

Bouncing on the ground

Take the best bouncing ball.
Use your hand as a surface
for the ball.
Press the ball down on your hand,
then let it go.
How does the ball change?
What can you feel as you let
the ball go?

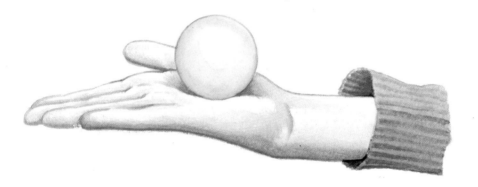

When a ball hits the hard ground the
bottom part of it is pushed up. The ball
then springs back into shape. This
pushes the ball away from the ground.
Press a ping pong ball down on
your thumb.
Listen to the sound it makes as it
springs back into shape!

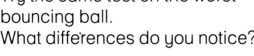

Try the same test on the worst
bouncing ball.
What differences do you notice?

Springy surfaces

First look at the set of balls which did
not bounce on a hard surface
(see page 20).
Would it make any difference if you
dropped them onto a springy surface?

Drop a marble onto different surfaces.
Which ones are best for making the
marble bounce?
Why does the marble bounce?

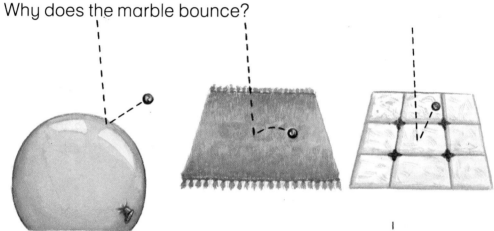

This time you can see the surface, not
the ball, changing shape.
The material springs back into shape,
pushing the marble away.

A marble will bounce better on some
surfaces than others. What does this
tell you about the surfaces?
You could use the marble to test how
springy they are.

Making sounds

Stretch out a rubber band and pluck it. What do you notice?

The rubber band makes a sound and moves quickly backwards and forwards.
This movement is called vibrating. Some musical instruments have springy strings. Sounds are made by the strings vibrating.
Make an instrument with rubber bands.

YOU NEED

a container which will not bend (a mug will do)
rubber bands

WHAT YOU DO

1. Stretch two or three rubber bands across the mug.

2. Pluck the bands to make them vibrate. Does each rubber band make the same sound?

Drums have a skin which is tightly stretched. Make a drum.

YOU NEED
a container which is round and will not bend
a piece of rubber sheeting or a balloon
rubber bands
pencils as drumsticks

WHAT YOU DO
1. Stretch the rubber skin across the container. Fix it in place with a rubber band.

2. Beat the skin and feel how springy it is.
Can you make a pencil bounce on the skin?
When you beat the skin it vibrates to make sounds.

3. Loosen the drum skin.
What difference do you notice in the sound?

The strings from a guitar can be made from coiled wire. The strings can be tightened, like the drum skin, to give the right sound.

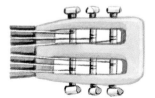

Springy power

The power in springy materials can be used to make things move.

YOU NEED

a washing-up liquid bottle
scissors
two pencils
a long rubber band

WHAT YOU DO

1. Take the cap off the bottle. Ask an adult to help you cut off the bottom of the bottle.

a clockwork toy

2. Get a long rubber band and loop it over a pencil.
Put the pencil across the top of the bottle.

3. Put your hand up inside the bottle and pull down the rubber band.
Loop this end over another pencil.
Two notches cut in the bottle will help keep this pencil in place.

a bow and arrow

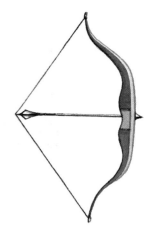

4. Turn the pencil at the top of the bottle to wind up the rubber band.
Then push the pencil in the other direction to start the rubber band unwinding.
Watch as the power in the rubber band turns the pencil.

Notes for teachers and parents

Children enjoy handling materials and finding out which ones bend, twist, stretch and spring. *Bounce, Stretch and Spring* explores the properties of these materials and their use in everyday life. Simple tests on the materials enable children to compare, measure and make predictions.

Page 4. Some children tend to think of stretchy materials as those which also spring back. Here their attention is drawn to materials which stretch, but do not return to shape. The terms 'elastic' and 'plastic', defining these properties, are not used here as they could be confused with the materials named elastic and plastic.

Pages 5, 6 and 7. The amount a material extends is in proportion to the pull on it. If the material is kept weighted it may go beyond the limit of elasticity and not return to shape. One leg of the pair of tights is kept unstretched as a 'control', a visual reference point for comparison.

Pages 8 and 9. Through experience children become aware of a relationship between stretch and pull. 'The more you pull (or the more marbles), the more it stretches.' They can then progress to quantifying that relationship. If a 100g weight, or 10 marbles, stretches the rubber band 2cm, a 200g weight, or 20 marbles, will stretch it 4cm, and so on up to the elastic limit. The tests are structured with one variable being changed at a time because children often find it difficult to identify and control the variables for themselves. They can be helped by discussing what they should do to make the test fair. Encourage children to try the tests several times and to look for any emerging pattern. They can observe that if the weight remains constant – a) twice the thickness of rubber band gives half the extension; b) twice the length gives twice the extension.

Pages 12 and 13. Making weighing machines gives the opportunity to make a scale and calibrate weights against it.

Page 17. If available, bath sealant can be used to demonstrate the function of cartilage.

Page 18. Writing on the balloon allows children to see how the surface of the balloon changes as it is stretched.

Pages 20–25. The bounciness of a substance depends upon its elastic recovery. When a ball hits a surface the energy of movement dents the ball, the surface, or both. How well the ball bounces depends on – a) the speed at which the energy is recovered; b) whether all the energy is returned, i.e., some could be lost in sound energy, heat energy or in altering the shape of the ball or surface.

Pages 26 and 27. Different sounds are produced by both the length and tension of strings.

Page 28. Energy is stored in the rubber band and released as it unwinds. The storing of energy can also be demonstrated by making the balloon jet (see *In the Air*, page 26).

Index and Glossary